REFLECTIONS BY BETHANY

REFLECTIONS BY BETHANY
POETRY, PRAYERS, AND LAUGHTER

BETHANY L. GOETHE

2020 Pages & Pie Publishing

Copyright © 2020 by Bethany L. Goethe

All rights reserved.

No part of this book may be reproduced in any form or by any electronic or mechanical means, including information storage and retrieval systems, without written permission from the author, except for the use of brief quotations in a book review.

ISBN 978-1-7359621-3-9

Library of Congress Cataloging-in-Publication Data

Goethe, Bethany.

Reflections by bethany: poetry, prayers, and laughter /Bethany L. Goethe.

Printed in the United States of America

Cover Art by Kristen Hubers

Cover Design by Karri Klawiter

Editing by Tiffany Avery and Angela Hammond Denny

Formatting by Angela Hammond Denny

DEDICATION

To my Dads (who have both passed into glory) and Moms for giving me such wonderful unconditional love and values that make me who I am today.

To my hubby Brian for being by my side always and being my best friend.

Kristen and Austin; Magnolia, Dylan, Pepper.

Keith and Stacy.

And furbabies; Sampson and Delilah, Sugaree and Eleanore.

CONTENTS

Foreword   ix

PART I
Poetry   1

1. A Day in My Life   3
2. Never Too Late   4
3. Never Alone   6
4. Whirling Thoughts   7
5. Your Song   8
6. Nevertheless   10
7. But a Moment   11
8. In Times of Sorrow   12
9. God's Blessings   14
10. Faith is an Open Door   15
11. Follow Your Own Path   16
12. Heave Ho, Heave Ho   18
13. Buck Up   19
14. If Only   20
15. I AM   22
16. What About You?   23
17. Stealing Prayers?   24
18. God the Lifesaver   25
19. Are You Ready?   26
20. Take Your Children to Church   28
21. Be Wholesome   30
22. Sing Today   31
23. Christmas Joy   32
24. Rest   34
25. Where is God?   35
26. Evil "Edna"   36
27. The Thyroid-Ectomy Thank You   38

PART II
Prayers   39

28. When I'm Afraid   41
29. In God's Arms   42
30. Stay Faithful   44
31. God Give Me Joy!   45
32. Take Away My Pharaoh's Heart   46
33. Only Believe   48
34. You Raise Us Up   50
35. Your Amazing Glory   51
36. Pure of Heart   52

PART III
Family   55

37. Thanks, Dad   57
38. Happy Father's Day!   58
39. I Love You, Mom   59
40. For My Husband   60
41. Daughter's Love   61
42. Love of a Teenage Son   62
43. Now a Marine   63
44. Child They'll Never Know   64

PART IV
Laughter   67

45. So Thoughtful of You   69
46. Morning is for the Birds   70
47. Vicks Vapor Rub   71
48. The Liver Laugh   72
49. Amusement Park Rides   73
50. Giggles!   74
51. Ten Tablespoons of Butter   75
52. Dream Words?   76
53. Chewed-Up Christmas Present   77
54. Are you Saying I'm Fat?   78
55. I Don't Wanna!   80

The End   81
Notes   83
Acknowledgments   87

FOREWORD

These poems were written to inspire, lift your spirit, and help you through hard times. Everyone at some point in their life comes to a time when they feel down and out. You may come to realize through times of sorrow, loneliness, pain, depression, or whatever the case may be, God has a plan for you. Times aren't always meant to be light and gleeful. God gives us the rain along with the sunshine so we can see He is the one we must turn to.

Many of these inspirational poems came to me in the middle of the night at a time when sleep wouldn't come. God would talk to me until I had to get out of bed and write down what He was saying. He is my inspiration! Sometimes it was on a day when there was no one else around and the loneliness was everywhere. Lots of times it was in the middle of a wonderful book, in the morning during my devotions, or after laughing with a friend or relative on the phone. And the funny poems were written because it's so much fun to just laugh and say something funny for the pure joy of it.

If even one of these poems can bring a smile to your face, make you whisper a prayer, or just plain cry out to God, then I praise God for giving these words to you.

Joy comes in the morning and Jesus comforts us when we mourn. Sometimes the only way He can speak to us is through our sadness. But don't forget either that the joy of the Lord is our strength, and our strength comes from serving Him!

Remember, there is a time for everything and a season for every activity under heaven.[1] Nothing is new, everything was here already, long ago before our time. God will call the past to account.[2] But thank God that Jesus covered all our past mistakes and failures with His love and mercy! You need only believe our Savior died on the cross and shed His precious blood so we could look to Him and see that He became the sacrificial lamb to make us free! Isn't that enough to make you want to giggle?

My prayer is that you will take the time to read and enjoy this, laugh, cry, be inspired, and share this book with others who may also need what one of these pages has to offer.

ENJOY!

PART I
POETRY

A DAY IN MY LIFE

I'm on my second cup of coffee
and sitting in my chair
by the table in the kitchen
with a head full of wet hair
My dog's lying outside
soaking up the sun
My mom and dad just called me
and we talked a ton
I have zucchini in my grinder
waiting to be mixed into bread
and I'm writing this poem
that's going round in my head
I have the Lord inside me
warming up my heart
My Christian radio is blasting
giving my day a good start
Joy comes in the morning
Rejoicing comes too
Do you know the Lord Jesus?
I'll be praying that you do

NEVER TOO LATE

It's late in the evening
I'm rolling around in my bed
My thoughts are all awry
swimming around in my head
I cannot sleep
The Lord is talking to my soul again
Come away with me my beloved
Write down your thoughts within
So I come to this room
and write what is in my heart
He wants me to tell you about Him
So I listen, I do my part
I want you to know what He tells me
I want you to know Him like I do
It's not too late to tell them, Beth
"Get up!" He says, "Let them know I love them too"
So here I am with this message
I'm giving it to you
Please give your heart to Jesus
since he's coming soon to take us above
It's never too late to trust Him
Open your heart to His call
Don't give in to the evil of this world
Immediately at the feet of God fall
Just kneel at the feet of our Savior
Follow that still small voice
Listen to Him when he calls you
Don't hesitate to make that choice
Ask Him to come into your heart and save you
Tell Him you believe He died on that cross for your sins
Don't doubt in your heart that He loved you enough
to suffer so you could have peace within

Because peace comes to you when you ask Him
to deliver you from your sin
Trust me, the weight will be off your shoulders
You'll laugh, then you'll cry, then you'll grin

NEVER ALONE

Snowflakes fall in the frigid air
Wind blows lightly through your hair
You walk alone amidst crimson skies
You're thinking that no one hears your sighs
But God is there holding you high
keeping you safe, warm, and dry
Don't think of the cold or how your feet slide
or the darkness around you
or how troubles abide
God reaches in and touches your heart
healing the hurting
right where it starts
Give your days to the Lord
walk in His love
His strength will help you soar
from those old troubles
Swiftly
Away
Like the wings of a dove

WHIRLING THOUGHTS

The wages of sin creep round my chin
They slither and slide and wreak havoc within
My heart is all charred; ugly and hard
I can't eat or sleep when I think I'm so evil
But thank goodness for me Jesus' gift makes me free
He died on the cross for this entire world's sin
Because I believe this, I have happiness again

YOUR SONG

What song flows from you?
It is one pleasing to God?
What talent do you give for Him
as you walk upon this sod?
Every word that proceeds out of your mouth
is a song that flows from your heart
Is it a cacophony of noise, or is it
soothing others as you go about?
Each one of us sings a song
whether we know it or not
We all vibrate from within
with praises, or sometimes with sin
What are you singing?
What comes from within?
Are you living for Jesus,
or is your heart full of sin?
Sing to the Master, why don't you
Let praises resound in your soul
For the Father is waiting
to touch you and to make you every bit whole
Let your voices be heard above many
sing to our God from above
Shout out His mercy
send out His love
We need to be still sometimes to hear His voice
We need to reflect God in our souls
By listening, in silence, you will hear Him
He will make you whole
Your soul will then vibrate with passion
you'll be sending out love and quiet praise
to the Father above who in His mercy
will listen to your voice that you raise
Does your heart long for the Master?

It will sing praises unheard
Look into the eyes of Jesus
Read His beloved dear Word
The Bible tells us the story
of His merciful and infamous love
that He alone can give us
That send us *His* songs from above

NEVERTHELESS

Nevertheless God, that comforteth those that are cast down, comforted us[1]
When you think that God's not there
in your heart, or anywhere,
He is only a whispered prayer away
He is waiting for you to bow down
to turn to Him
To cast your burden of doubt and fear to the ground
God will give you nevertheless when you
just can't go on
When you fall at His feet and give Him your all
then you will know you were never alone
God heard your call
We need to lay our burdens at His feet
before He can do one thing
He needs to know we trust Him
to make our faith complete
So come to Him with your sorrows,
your burning hurts and woes
He will throw them far away and take you in His arms
You'll feel better from your head to your toes

BUT A MOMENT

Each day is but a moment
We live them one by one
so when grief comes to disrupt them,
we are overcome
Sorrow comes upon us
filling us with woe
bursting our bubbles of happiness,
confusing what we know
It's so hard to lose a loved one,
who is so close to our heart
someone who is so dear
with whom we never want to part
Time can't erase our sadness
or make that loved one return
but on memories you will reflect
and on joyful moments sojourn
So while you go through this journey
which will almost certainly take a while to rise above
meditate on happy days gone by
and remember this dear one with love
Each day will start getting better
and sorrow will soon start to end
because you'll have those precious memories
and then you'll be able to mend

IN TIMES OF SORROW

Life is but a moment
Handle it with care
Do God's will and spend
lots of time in prayer
Life has many trials
that will devastate
But when you lift your heart to Jesus
He will help you wait
Wait when trials come to overwhelm you
Wait upon the Lord
Get on your knees before Him
Look into His Word
There will be much wisdom
in this book of love
Jesus also had difficulties
but looked to His Father God above
There were times He had to wait
like when He was in the desert
for 40 days He wandered there
It definitely was not pleasant!
Right now you're going through sorrow
It's hard to see what's just around the bend
But now while each day passes,
rely on the love of your family and Friend
You have a friend in Jesus
He'll be the entire world to you
He'll help you through this lonely time
and hold you in His arms too
Read Psalm 91 and bask
in the promise of God's Word
To keep you safe under His feathers
and give you blessings yet unheard
Each tomorrow will be a little better

Don't give up or look at the bad
God's angels are all around you
They know why you are sad
But they also know your departed one
is quite alive in heaven above
Surrounded not only by God's presence,
but by happiness, joy, peace, and love

GOD'S BLESSINGS

May God's blessings be upon you
as you go forth on this day
May His will be ever on you
as you kneel down to pray
May your hearts swell up with joy
every time you sing His praises
because you know God loves you
and His blessings still amaze us
We are all God's children,
His handiwork of love
With each morning's sunrise
come His blessings from above
We watch in awed silence
at His majestic signs so bold
And realize His mercies
as we receive one more day foretold
Each day's a new beginning
We get to start again anew
Thus, we realize God's faithfulness
and His patience with us too
So thank God for His glory
Thank Him when you pray
Sing a happy hallelujah
and dance the day away

FAITH IS AN OPEN DOOR

Faith is an open door to the Father up above
Nails didn't hold our Father's hands in place,
but His enduring, unselfish love
Walk to God each day in scriptures so profound
Open up your faith by kneeling on God's holy ground
Worship God in spirit and in truth sublime
Drink in His presence by reading God's letter of love and spending time
with our precious Savior and taking time to pray, worship, and adore Him
before we go our way
Into the unforgiving work world and shades of uncaring gray
that seem to draw our hearts from Jesus and carry our minds astray
We all can get like Thomas[1] with our thoughtless doubts and fears,
but when we take that daily time with our Savior
He wipes away all our worrisome fear
with His calm and blessed assurance that indeed *Jesus is mine*[2]
Like in that precious old hymn we sing about
giving us a foretaste of God's glory so divine
So, work in the Word of Jesus, take time to walk with Him and pray
then God will lift away your doubts
so you'll have a better day

FOLLOW YOUR OWN PATH

Each of us must follow our own path
into places unknown
our eyes blinded to the promises
that through God only can be shown
In the course of time you will see
what valleys of shadows
you will come across
and what must be
But when you go through your valley
that seems so dark and drear,
hold on to the promise of salvation
and keep faith forever near
God will never leave us nor forsake us[1]
so He has promised in His Word
even when the way is scary,
He'll give us a way out like the wings of a bird
to fly away from our own terror
that endeavors to track us down
trying to compel us into the shadows
to take away our crown
The crown God promises to give us
if we kneel down in surrender at His throne
Giving our hearts to Him only
this makes His salvation our own
Then He'll show us the approach to a pathway
that leads to His throne above
making us want to obey Him
and follow this new direction of love
Love that compels us to tell these promises
to a world of weary travelers who are going the wrong way
Following the worldwide highway of evil
which leads from our God away
to a wide path that's easy to follow

Since you do what is safe and allowed
because everyone does it they tell you
So you just tag along with the crowd
We'll be able to talk to those people
who feel so all alone
wondering where their peace and joy is
why it's the darkest day they've ever known
We'll be able to stop them
before they take a leap off the nearest bridge
because Jesus died on the Cross
to forgive all our sins and even made us a pledge
He'll never leave nor forsake us
He'll be there by our sides
to conquer all our fears
that in the darkness seems to hide
He'll chase away our demons
for He is the truth and the light[2]
and when we ask Him for forgiveness,
the dark shadows of fear will turn to daylight
He'll give you a new path to glory
and make you feel so brand new
that you'll want to follow Him always
and tell all your friends too
But like I said in the beginning,
the path for the Lord is tough
just keep walking on that path of light
because that light and love is ENOUGH

HEAVE HO, HEAVE HO

Throw out the bait and let it go
into the ocean and out to the sea
for the love of God is leading me
to learn the scriptures
and bring loved ones in
from the all-time low
of the lure of sin
Give God your heart
Live for the Lord
Open the Bible
Dive into His Word
For God's Word is a lamp
to make it easy to see
when the going is dark
it sets our tangled feet free
For the wages of sin
try to trip us within
but God's Word opens the door
and lets the light in

BUCK UP

Stick out your chin
Today is a new page
In this book of life you're living in
Grab on to hope
Don't let it go
Plant determination in your heart
Walk forward, clamp on to that prize
Even if the going is slow
You are a winner
Fight for your goal
Try out new things
Jump over that hole
of indecision and defeat
gloom or despair
Don't be defeated
Get out of that chair
You need to step forward
You need to begin
Strive for the success that will help you win
You are an achiever
You are a prize
You can do it
Everyone will see it in your eyes
You know what you can do
God gave you all the talent to proceed
He knows when you are feeling low
And He perceives your every need
So jump on the band wagon
We all know you can
It's time for you to believe in yourself
and make a new plan

IF ONLY

If only is an open door
to an empty mind
Fill your mind with conscience thought
so that it will soon unbind
If only are just two words
Step out into the unknown
"If only I could do this or that"
can become wings to spaces yet unfound
So open your mind
Put one foot in front of the other
or grab a hand
ask your friend or brother
It may take a day,
a week, or a year
But you need to get out
release all your fear
We are all in this world
to do the "if only"
If we don't do it
someone else will make the money
Don't take too long
to decide what to do
because there are others
just like you
who say "if only I could
be here or there"
Then think to themselves,
"you can if you dare"
Well just do the if only
Jump in that driver's seat
Step off of that ladder
of indecision and defeat

Get into the water
Paddle with all you can
Pretty soon you will find
the "if only" *was* a good plan

I AM

I AM[1] is love
I AM has sent you and me, so
go into the entire world and preach for Him
I AM is our shepherd
We are His sheep
His sheep know I AM's voice
We are God's chosen people,
so let love be your greatest aim
I AM brings joy
The joy of the Lord is our strength
Fear of the Lord is the beginning of wisdom
Joy comes in the morning
Every day is a new beginning,
so use it wisely, start with God
Don't even imagine that you can do anything without love
Again, let love be your greatest aim
We are the heirs of God
He is the tree of life[2]
we get our nourishment from His Word
Let us be generous with this knowledge
Give us this day our daily bread,[3] I AM,
so we may follow through with works of peace
Help us walk in that peace today
so the words of our mouth and the meditation
of our hearts will be acceptable to You, I AM
Our sins are forgiven as far as the east is from the west,[4]
so be anxious for nothing, give your all to God
But always remember what we do for God matters forever,
and our faithfulness on this Earth has eternal consequences
I AM *is* the A to Z, the beginning and the end
I AM will give to everyone according to what he or she has done[5]
So, get busy and remember, you don't have to feel like a leader to lead
and today is the tomorrow we worried about yesterday

WHAT ABOUT YOU?

Are you willing to risk your life for Jesus?
Do you want to do His will?
Even if it takes doing it alone?
What are you searching for?
Is it truth? In the Bible it says:
I am the way and the truth and the life
No one comes to the Father, if not by me[1]
Who is this one speaking?
This is Jesus. He died on the cross for our sins
Do you believe this?
If you do, then you are ready to go to heaven
Will you tell others?
Don't be afraid, there are others in this world
who need Christ just as much as you do
Sometimes, it's not just telling others but showing them
by the way you live
What about you?
What have you done for Jesus?
What will you do for Jesus?
What are you waiting for?
Time is of the essence
Go ye into all the world, and preach the gospel[2]
Yes, but if we all do our part in our own little space
Then that is what that scripture means
Right?
Jesus is coming soon

STEALING PRAYERS?

No one can take away my prayers from me
Here I am Lord; I'm not always down on my knees
I pray every day
It's in my head
Twenty-four hours those prayers are said
What were you thinking Madalyn Murray O'Hair?
Who told you that you could take away prayer?
You were just a small vessel
a Satanic pawn,
a tinkling symbol,
a mere cumbersome yawn
Don't let anyone fool you, Christian
Our prayers are not dead
Pray twenty-four seven like I do
in my heart, in my head!
God knows my thoughts
God knows my prayers
I teach in the schools
and I pray when you're not aware
Look out,
Here they come
My prayers will not stop
I'll pray every day
till the day I drop

GOD THE LIFESAVER

I am a writer with a message to give,
but not one of blessing if without Christ you live
Mercy is from God who gave us His son
He is the answer, He is the one
Believe that God's son on the cross, His life He gave,
if you refuse to believe, your soul He can't save
Save you ask? I don't understand
Well, He is our Savior and His death was all part of God's plan
He came to this Earth to warn us of sin
to heal our diseases; to give us peace within
But peace only comes when you answer His call
You receive His message and give Him your all
So look up to Jesus
Bring Him your cares
Lay them down at the cross
Walk up those stairs
You cannot be complacent, the time is right now
Give the Lord your heart and receive His solemn vow
that if you kneel at His cross and believe in His name
trust in His mercy, and know that He came
He died on that cross so that we might live
If we look to Him for our salvation,
salvation He will give
So say in your heart
oh Lord, I confess,
I am a sinner, I live in duress
Without You, I'm nothing
With You, I'm free
Jesus, I believe You died to save me
The blood you shed on Calvary's cross[1] that long ago day
takes every one of the sins I committed away
Your love is everlasting, infinite, and free
By believing in You, I am saved for eternity

ARE YOU READY?

I'm mourning the loss of the freedom we once had
My heart feels fear for a world on the verge of going bad
But no matter what, you still have one day
Use it wisely for the Lord
before our freedoms are taken away
"One Nation under God"[1]
will no longer be said?
Abortion will be easier
Women will mourn the loss of their dead
Change is coming
Not always a good thing
Get your heart right with the Lord
His praises to sing
The Israelis stood up to the Egyptians
Putting lambs' blood on their doors[2]
We need to kneel like Daniel,[3] no matter what
with our knees on the floors
Let us change our hearts
let us change our wills
times will get tougher
But God will give us a way out still
Put Him first in your life
Don't keep Him out in the cold
Change your heart for God
Stand up now and be bold
Only God knows the hour
and the day Jesus will come
So give your heart to Him
right now, don't be dumb
Things might look good right now
but soon they will get bleak
Stand up and count for Jesus
Get off your duffs and speak

Speak up, stand tall, resist what's bad
Don't let our future heirs be sad
Do what you can before it's too late
so your heart will be ready
when you meet God at His Pearly Gate

TAKE YOUR CHILDREN TO CHURCH

I saw a little boy in church the other day
He was giving his mother trouble
because he didn't want to be there
He wanted to go home and play
The mother was beside herself
trying to keep the boy still,
trying to hear God's message,
trying to do God's will
The little boy kept complaining,
crying, wiggling, making noise
Until the vexed mother disciplined him
the way mothers will do to little boys
God gives us little children
to satisfy our hearts
when we were so very lonely,
longing for a new start
Just remember that children
are precious gifts from God
They're here to accompany us in this world
to travel with us on this sod
So give your hearts to Jesus
Teach your children His word
You will be so happy
when your child's heart reaches out to God
They may be naughty in church sometimes
but everyone understands
We're sitting in front and behind you
smiling and "holding his hand"
Everyone loves little children
Don't worry that they'll fuss in the pew,
because everyone knows that someday
they will be standing straight and tall beside you
Because you have chosen the right path,

to bring your child to the Lord's house
That child will eventually follow God's way
with his children and spouse
So give your children to Jesus
Bring them into God's room
Teach them the scriptures and love them
because that's the right thing to do

BE WHOLESOME

A saucy look
A pert swift nod
A wicked electric attraction
Veers your path away from God
Oh those clothes look so sassy
Those full lips turned down into a pout
That sexy twinkle in her eyes
Makes you just want to shout
"Oh yes, I'll go with you honey"
Her charm is so easy to swallow
She'll wrap her arms tightly around you
Her wicked path is so easy to follow
But God made just one woman for you
You must remember that, son
There is just one path to heaven
and your journey has just begun
There are so many easier pathways,
so many women with their different charms
But if you stay close to the Savior,
He'll lead the right one into your arms
He'll show you His will if you'll let Him
He'll open the doors of your hearts
He'll lead you both to each other
with an astounding love that will in no way depart
But if that saucy, pert woman
gets you into her snare,
you won't be able to escape her
She'll be your downfall, for she doesn't care
Of course, the right woman will be a Christian
She may not be rich or drive a fancy car
but she'll understand you and love you
You'll both be happy with each other just as you are

SING TODAY

The Lord is our shepherd,[1] leader, and guide
Put your faith in Him and He'll be by your side
Don't worry or fear as the Bible does say
when things may look bleak and the sky may be gray
Turn your eyes to our Father, our comfort, our friend
Put your hand in His and He'll be with you till the end
Wonder no more what tomorrow may bring
Tomorrow is later, today we must sing
Worship with joy and reach out to each other
Do what you can for your sister and brother
They may not be real family or relatives to you,
but God knows their hearts and wants you to know them too
So don't just walk by without saying a word
Look into their eyes and let them know Jesus is Lord
Treat them with love; be good-hearted and kind
And together with God's help your goodness will shine
Your brother or sister will feel they belong
They'll want to come back to this family of believers
Joining in with us to worship our Savior
and become our family as well
together with their own heavenly song

CHRISTMAS JOY

The bells ring in the city
people fill the square
Shoppers buying presents
because God's spirit is there
It's time to rejoice
look into the face of others
Smile with warmth
take time to listen, forgetting what bothers
Pray about what gifts to give
Do a kind act for a friend
Release your heart from poverty
by having love's tenderness within
Hearts will open like flowers
when kind words are spoken to them
making them want to respond in kind
by sending you back a sweet grin
Scientists may wonder,
don't hearts just pump blood?
Not only that, you thinkers,
our hearts can fill up with love
When the chambers of your heart feel empty
then your soul may resonate with hate
But when love enters your heart forever
it pushes from it all the charred slate
So, give your heart to Jesus
He's the lover of your soul
Go ahead and beam at your brother, child
then your faith will begin to grow
Don't think about what this world can give you
It's empty with promises that can't deliver one thing
Watch and see, don't you still feel empty
after the holidays' unfulfilling fling?
When you can reach out to others

and share the elation of your heart
Only then will you feel totally fulfilled
by the possession of love that can never depart
So ring the bells of Christmas
Send out a warm smile or a hug
Listen to each other's hearts,
instead of emanating a frown or a stare or a shrug
Merry Christmas everybody
My heart is fulfilled, it's true
I'm sending you a present
This heartfelt poem for you

REST

The rivers of life
may consume your very soul
When fear comes in and grabs
to try to steal your soul
There's nothing in this world
that can keep you from those valleys
Where thoughts of self-hatred flow
and creep into the alleys
Your mind perceives confusion
Your heart may feel no love
The swimming hole of life feels shallow
when empty hollow chasms shove
Desolation leaves a blankness
Our hope in life feels gone
But there is living water just ahead
Fall to your knees and carry on
There is the one who will adore you
the one who knows you best
Pray to Him, His name is Jesus
come to Him and you'll find rest

WHERE IS GOD?

When your heart splits in two
When nobody is around and
you don't know what to do
When tragedy strikes,
a loved one dies
Why does the sun still come out
when you think it has no right to shine
When you are still so angry and out of your mind
When nothing feels right it's all so intense, so unkind
Your mind shuts down, its ready to blow
Your feet won't move, your body says "No!"
WHERE IS GOD?
Things feel so dismal for days on end
You just can't cope, where is your best friend?
Your faithful friend
God has been here, right here all along
bearing your burden, hearing your sad song
He quietly waits in your heart, your inner man
waits until you're ready to turn to Him again
He knows your pain, He feels your tears
He's been there all along and has been for years

EVIL "EDNA"

Once there was a woman name "Edna"
who was not a nice lady at all
She put her own mother in a nursing home
so all the money would be at her beck and call
Her family was quite dysfunctional
because she was an over-controlling freak
Her husband ran away also
leaving her only to shriek
"I'll have it all, mind you
I'll stand aside for no man
I am, I say"
All were under her command
At her beck and call, everyone turned crazy and gray
Finally, the Lord returned for His faithful servants
They all disappeared and none were left around
Save control freaking "Edna"
who stared up at God with a frown
His face was so full of pity
She knew she'd be left to face evil, Satan, and shame
Belatedly, she regretted how awful she'd been at her self-seeking game
but now life as she knew it was over, winter for her had finally come
She'd face her own trepidations feeling horribly miserable and numb
Oh children will you be like "Edna," evil to the core?
Never having quite enough, always wanting more?
Screaming, fighting, kicking, and trying to get your own way
until no one likes you and your heart is all charred and decayed
Won't you turn to Jesus and give Him all this worldly lust
Things that make you greedy, which will only in the end turn to rust
The world's gold is only God's pavement in heaven
Why not just leave it here
You can't bring it with you when you die[1]
That message is quite loud and clear

So turn to Jesus, because unfortunately we're all a little like "Edna"
He is the lover of your soul
He will change your evil heart if only you'll kneel before Him
and ask God to be in control

THE THYROID-ECTOMY THANK YOU

Kathy, who has a ready smile and chipper attitude for everyone to see
Lisa, who helped me with all her knowledge about thyroidectomies
Talking to me while being supportive throughout the night
Her perceptive approach dissipated all my thryroid-ectomy fright
Diane was the angel nurse who helped me wash my hair
She helped me with my meds and treated me with great care
Her words of knowledge meant much to me
as they took away any confusion about medical jargon debris
Another nurse one night helped me after I heaved and spewed
She patiently cleaned up the mess without becoming unglued
We then talked about our families later on and I hated to see her go,
but her shift ended without me finding out her name – Oh no
Dr. P came in to see me and my hubby later on that day
with his sparkling eyes and huge grin, making us both giggle
yet passing on brilliant knowledge within minutes, I'd say less than ten
Beautiful Sarah was very helpful, happy, and in control
She made us feel very comfy while busy-ness took its toll
I cannot forget my surgeon, Dr. H, either
Without his expert service I'd still be sporting a goiter bigger than ever
His knowledge, prayers, and skill sure saved me from distress
Now I can get on with life and live again in happiness
There were the quick-witted and fun nurses,
who wheeled me down the hall,
brought me to the anesthesiologist who was busier than them all
She and Dr. H explained my surgery to me well
Then before I knew it, I was awake listening to a nurse
humming a song of which I could not tell
But her sweet and happy attitude was
comforting and made me feel swell
Well, there you have it
My stay at the hospital was a lot less painful than it could have been
Because of you wonderful dutiful workers there acted much more like friends

PART II
PRAYERS

WHEN I'M AFRAID

Dear Lord, help me remember when I feed my fears I lose sight of You
What ifs, should haves, how will I do this or that
cannots, closed doors, steep mountain terrains
keep my poor mind in a stew
These fears wake me up in the middle of the night,
filling my mind with horrible fright
"Oh God," I pray, "what will I do?"
Then He speaks to my heart softly and I climb out of bed
Going to my quiet place where His Holy Word is read
These scriptures inspire me all over again and help me anew
To see that He loves me and the scriptures are true
He takes those dreaded fears right out of my brain
and my heart starts to sing a whole new refrain
The Lord has not given me the spirit of fear[1]
He won't leave or forsake me, for the Holy Spirit is near[2]
Jesus died on the cross and took my place
His blood set me free to live in His grace
So make up your mind to follow His will, you can live in fear or just be still
Listen to God when He's speaking to you
That still small voice[3] is wisdom
taking the blame that ole devil wishes to devise
which produces fear too
So look into the Word and fill your mind again
With words of wisdom from the Lord which keep you from sin

IN GOD'S ARMS

I look out in wonderment at the sun
shining its rays on a still, frozen Earth
dazzling specks of frost dance and shimmer on the windows
whips and swirls of snow in a lackadaisical pattern of whispering beauty
I sense the calming effects of this scene coming over my soul
just knowing that I am safe and warm inside
makes me thankful for my home
A hawk flies past and I wonder at its fortitude
How does it survive in this frigidness?
What must it do to endure and maintain its life right
now while I am safe inside?
I think back to when I was young and had not a care in the world
my parents always watching over me to make sure no harm came to me
How the Lord must look over this lone hawk
and all the other animals in this world
Everything has a place in the world,
there is a time and a season for everything[1]
One day this hawk will no longer be here nor will I,
but for now, there is a reason I am here glancing out the window
noticing what God has placed on this Earth for my pleasure
I thank God for what He has given us, do you?
Count your blessings, sing songs of praise,
and worship the Lord in His holiness
be grateful for what He has given us
and treasure this artistic paintbrush of love
Do you ever observe the hand of God in the clouds?
A majestic sunrise or sunset,
a rainbow gleaming with brilliant colors after rain?
The powerful strokes of lightning in a dark sky,
billions of stars twinkling on a calm clear night?
Or the waves washing up on the seashore after a storm?
The deer quietly nibbling in the fields
listening to the wind whisper

while the fields of grass hide the little field mice
scurrying to feed their young
The Psalms declare Your majesty Oh Lord
Job speaks of the wonderment You have created
The Earth declares Your voice of prophetic beauty
every single moment in time
I praise the name of the Lord and worship You in Your holiness
Thank you, Lord for all that You have given us
there is so much more to say
to see
to be
For this I thank You, praise You, worship You
Your voice whispers to me in the beauty of your creation
It speaks volumes to me through the mighty prophecies in the sword,
which are Your scriptures You have given us to read
The sword of the spirit will guide me through all the paths that I must trod
I am here
I am listening, trusting, worshipping, and praising You
in the beauty of Your holiness
Thank you, God, for Your gifts of love
that will last until the end of time

STAY FAITHFUL

May the glory of the Lord attend to us
as we go throughout the course of this day
Let our lips proclaim Your faithfulness
in the most fulfilling way
Let our knees bow in humbleness
and reverence enrapture our soul
Let us rely on Your unfailing mercies
and be confident of Your righteous control
That gives us the blessed assurance
that Your love is complete and entire
We will never need worry
that Your spirit won't be our total desire
So let us come into Your presence
and sing the song "Jesus is Mine!"[1]
Oh what a foretaste of heaven
when God's will is totally thine

GOD GIVE ME JOY!

I love to tell Your story
even when it hurts
My heart has continually been broken
by the devil's accusing words
Sometimes I cannot take it
My heart feels all broken down
It's hard to handle life, Lord
when my head's so low to the ground
Oh come take all the pieces
and fill my heart again
Quickly mend my fences
and my defenses defend
I am all Yours, Lord
I want to do Your will
Open my heart and fill it
with Your love, strength, and mend
my broken heart from sorrow
my wounded soul within
Take away the sadness
give me joy again

TAKE AWAY MY PHARAOH'S HEART

Replace it, Lord, with Yours
No more procrastination, compromise, or insincere repentance
to keep me from your shores
I want to be Your bride, dear Lord
come into my heart
Give me love, joy, peace, and patience, Lord
right from the very start
Let each day be new with Your love
Let me read Your Word
Come into my heart, dear Lord
giving me wisdom from the tree of life[1]
the most sustaining promise ever heard
You died on that tree so long ago
to give me the promise of life from above
Thank you, Lord, for what You have done
by Your precious, redeeming, unselfish love
Come into my heart each day
let me fulfill Your plan
Give me the love that You have, Lord
to take to this human clan
Your love sustains us, gives us hope
from the pressures of this life
Take away our worries, Lord
our pressures and our strife
By Your Word we'll read each day
as we take time in the morn
That You gave Your followers what You had planned
to fulfill Your prophecies from God
Come into all our hearts
Renew Your promise in us
Let us go into this world
to demonstrate Your love so wondrous,
Your precious plan from above

Fulfill Your will in our hearts, dear Lord,
make us new each day
That we may share the love You gave
as we go on our way
To climb the narrow pathway upwards
that You alone have trod
Let us show that no one cares for us like You,
the precious son of God

ONLY BELIEVE

Clang! Clang! Clang!
The echoes of hammering filled the air
wails of horror, wails of sorrow
Mary, His mother, clumped over in agony
"My Son! My Son! Oh God, My son!
Jesus! Jesus! Jesus!"
The cross was raised up
Tender flesh ripped open
"Why Father?! Why?" He cried[1]
Never-the-less, He forgave
Father, forgive them; for they know not what they do[2]
He refused the legions of angels
who would have come if He had given up
But He didn't
Imagine that
That's why He is our Savior
Thank you, Jesus
You died to set us free
And now we are free to leave our burdens of sin at the foot of the cross
Where You are waiting to take them
and remove all sorrow from our hearts that this sin causes
We praise you, Jesus
Thank you, Lord for giving us hope in this world of sin
Come into my heart, Lord Jesus
Rise up new followers every day
Show them that God is love
We don't have to follow a set of rituals to be saved
From our sin, from our guilt, from our past
We need only believe
You died to take away the sin of the world
You had mercy on us, and still do
You are not willing that ANY should perish,
but that all should come to repentance

before You come back to bring us to heaven
Come into my heart and stay, Lord Jesus
Forever I will worship You
You gave your life so that we may live
Precious Savior and Lord
Amen! Come, Lord Jesus

YOU RAISE US UP

I raise You up in songs of glory
I raise You up in blessing Your name in praise
I raise You up to tell Your story
I raise You up, I raise You up
The Lord knows my heart
He knows who I am
With you I share my faith
I am not scared
Lift up your hands, give Him your heart
Share your faith, come away, and come apart
from the evil of this world,
from the doubt in your mind
Give your all to Jesus
Come out of the darkness and the daily grind
You raise us up to praise Your glory
You raise us up to sing Your praise
You raise us up to tell Your story
You raise us up, You raise us up

YOUR AMAZING GLORY

The amazing power of God's love flows through us
It is bound up in our very veins
Our hearts pump out hallelujahs
Joy flows from our hearts to our brains
The words rush out in fountains
from our lips and tongue we sing Your praise
Glory, glory, hallelujah
Your joy is in this place
We'll never understand Your mercy
Our hearts can only feel the joy
Our arms shoot up towards heaven
Our lips rejoice in song
Praise You Holy Father
Thank You for Your love
You alone can save us
from Your heavenly throne above
We worship and adore You
We will dance with joy before You
You amaze us with Your glory
Thank you
Thank You for Your salvation story

PURE OF HEART

Your heart is as pure as snow
The Lord has helped you keep it so
I think of lilies of the valley
when I think of you
A precious child of God so true
Keeping your heart pure
is sometimes hard to do
But when you stay close to Jesus,
He will watch over you
Open His Word daily
Drink in those words of truth
You will never then be lonely
His presence will wash over you
He'll keep you in His arms
as in Psalms 91
(whenever you get scared or lonely,
just read that Psalm for fun)
You'll always have a friend in Jesus
when you keep His Word and
follow His commands
You will live long and flourish
because He'll be there to hold your hand
Some days you may find you want to give up
Some days you may need to cry
But when Jesus is your Savior
He'll always give you more strength to try
So start out every morning
whispering prayers to God above
Thanking Him for heaven
Praising Him for His love
Jesus will never leave you
even when this world is so cold
Ask Him to teach and guide you

while you share your faith so bold
When you keep on courageously following Him
He'll be there to hold your hand
when you follow in His footsteps
He'll be there to lift you out of sand
So keep your eyes on Jesus
He's watching over you
Your heart will be forever pure
Because your faith in Him will stay true

PART III
FAMILY

THANKS, DAD

Oh father of mine
whose arms held me tight
You keeper of goodness,
you lover of light
You walked in the darkness
with my hand held fast
so I wouldn't be afraid
or dwell on fears long passed
You still assure me in troubles
and pray night and day
I look for your comfort
when everything's gray
You see through the storms
You know what to do
I love and I care and sure respect you
You fall asleep reading God's Holy Word,
for the Lord is your keeper and shepherd
in this troublesome world
You've taught me to love Him
and follow His call
by your outstanding example
and by giving your all
Thanks, Dad

HAPPY FATHER'S DAY!

Wonders never cease
whenever you're around
You always make us laugh
but seldom make us frown
You always start the day
cheerful and alert
Your attitude is happy,
lighthearted, energetic, and pert
"Good morning, Sunshine,"
you say to everyone
Making us all feel joy
as you wake up with the sun
You set a good example
for all of your family and everyone
Because you always keep God in your heart,
and you love us, every one
What a wonderful Dad you are
We all look up to you
because you always share your wisdom
and give good advice too
Thanks, Dad, for being so special
we hope this day is grand
because you deserve the best
in the whole entire land
Happy Father's Day every day

I LOVE YOU, MOM

My Dearest Mom,
whom I love with all my heart
You are such a blessing
and have been from the start
I wish everyone had a mom like you
because your love for me always pulls me through
Those hard times that sap my brain
when Satan thinks he's got me on his chain
You just say a prayer for me
Then God and His precious angels of mercy
are there to set my "rattled chain" free
You lift up my spirit when it gets low
when a dish smashes to the floor, or I stub my toe
When the day doesn't go right or
I've gained a pound or two,
you don't hold that against me
That's why I love you
You give me support whenever I cry
you always remove that speck in my eye[1]
When the night falls around me and
I'm too scared to move,
your prayers seem to reach me
and help me to somehow get through
"The Lord is your shepherd,"
you say with a grin
I hear what you're saying
and walk away from all sin

FOR MY HUSBAND

Oh my sweet honey,
you're the man of my dreams
You make my heart happy
and it bursts at the seams
You are giving and caring,
unselfish, and kind
I love you so much
You are such a great find
I wouldn't trade you
no, never, no
You are my lover
you make my heart grow
You take all the hurt
out of my soul
Whenever I'm grieving
or feeling low
You never complain
when you listen to me
Your insight is painstakingly forthright and free
Please, don't ever leave me
My heart you revive
Without you, my love,
I would never survive

DAUGHTER'S LOVE

Our precious daughter, curly, long, flowing hair
Bouncy, energetic,
makes you want to stare
at her beauty
also bountiful within,
the way that she talks
makes you want to grin
Our precious daughter is everyone's own
We all love the way
you have totally grown
from a girl to a woman,
from a child to an adult
You know how to transform a place from tumult
Your happiness flows from the inside out
Making the room colorful
with artistic clout
The power you bring
when you step into a room
changes the atmosphere from the once dismal gloom
You are bright, terrifically talented, creative, and sure
Your smile shines within you,
and your world is secure
You know what you want
you bring with you such glee
I am so glad that you are related to me

LOVE OF A TEENAGE SON

You are as precious as the day is long
When I think of you,
I smile and sing a song
You bustle through this life
with loud music and your friends
But when I ask you to do a favor,
you take it with a grin
The music bongs right through you,
as you go your merry way
But deep inside your soul,
I know you know God's way
Sometimes you get upset
and scare away the dog
But inside it's a different story
You follow the paths of our God

NOW A MARINE

Our son's going overseas to Japan
He's no longer a teen
He has become a man
As soon as he goes,
we will miss him so
But we will see a change
he will start to grow
from the inside to the out
No longer misunderstood,
turning from the path of a teen
to that of manhood
Go with God, our son
take our Lord with you
Let Him lead your paths
and keep Him in your view
The wages of sin are death
Follow in God's way
Then wherever you may go
He'll be in your heart to stay

CHILD THEY'LL NEVER KNOW

They were just seventeen then,
young and all alone
Both of them in college and
far away from home
Nothing could stop the bondage
of loneliness and fear
Whenever he kissed her, she felt safe
in his arms, she was filled with cheer
Then one thing led to another,
they found themselves in love
They believed nothing could impede the passion
that no one could stop this obsession
But then she ended up pregnant,
boy was she terrified! No one knew
Tell her parents? She didn't dare
So yeah, you guessed it
They ended that precious little existence
and lived with years of regret
of being a murderer
at a standstill with that strife
Years have passed since that fated day
Both now are old and going gray
Time heals all wounds you say?
Nope! Think again! They still lament that day
Nearly every morning awoken with the thought
that child would be an adult right now
If only, what were we thinking? OW!
The heartache never goes away
living carries on with regret for what they had done
It could have been a daughter,
or it could have been a son
Children have been born since then

Their lives have blessed them so
But their hearts still ache for the other
The one they'll never know

PART IV
LAUGHTER

SO THOUGHTFUL OF YOU

Thank you for the thank you
it meant so very much
We got it in the mail
It had just the right touch
The words you wrote inside it
made us cry with sentimental glee
So when your card came to our eyes,
we had to cop a see
Just a few little words
turned our heads around
We danced all around the room
until we fell upon the ground
So the words in that special card
made us a happy dancing couple
We're glad you liked the money,
sent us that card of "Thank you"
and went to all that trouble

MORNING IS FOR THE BIRDS

The day commences yet again
The sun comes up
The barn swallow's conversations begin
Menageries of them are perched on the roof of our barn
Noisily conversing in groups of alarm
"Last night, Matilda, a cat crept into view
getting closer and closer to my nest
What was I to do?
So I pecked him, Matilda
That's what I did
The nerve of that cat going after my kid"
And so the conversations go
till 8 o'clock in the morning or so
Birds in the trees, on the roofs
talking, reverberating, waking,
giving us proof
That morning has indeed started
We no longer can sleep
These noisy birds' conversations
Creeping into slumber once deep
Cats are fast asleep now
We are wide awake
Matilda's child is safe
Now our children cry,
"Start the breakfast mom,
I want a pancake"

VICKS VAPOR RUB

Vicks, my mom's remedy
used since she was born
"Vicks works," she says
Slather it all over you
Do it! Don't be stubborn
Put it in your ear
When there is an ache
Stick it on dry skin
so that it won't flake
Rub it on a hemorrhoid
to relieve the pain
Do you have arthritis?
Put it on your joints before it rains
Has your foot fallen off?
Place it on the stub
"Maybe it'll grow back," she says
It's the magic of the eucalyptus rub
Do you have a nose that's stuffed?
A ligament out of joint?
A torn-off nail that's in the quick?
Yes, that is just the point
Get the Vicks and slather it on
The vapor will heal you
Do it now, don't be in pain
It's a remedy tried and true

THE LIVER LAUGH

Did you ever have the liver laugh?
The kind that never stops?
Your liver quivers with delight
You laugh until you drop
The liver laugh cures all your ills
It takes away swine flu
It cures all poisons taken in
that the doctors prescribe to you
Liver laugh until you cry
Laugh until you're blue
Laugh, laugh, laugh, and then laugh again
Your liver will thank you
Just laughing seventeen minutes a day
Will make you live much longer
Your liver will thank you very much
and your body will be stronger
Then, never will you be the same
Your innards will be merry
For your liver will be cured and
you'll feel as youthful as a rosebud cherry

AMUSEMENT PARK RIDES

Flip! Flop
Your stomach will drop
The ride goes way up
then comes to a stop
Now down, down, down,
as fast as can be
So fast your hands grab the bars
It doesn't matter what your eyes can see
Intense is the word
Carefree you feel
Giddy, heady, emotional zeal
Round the corner
Zip! Over the bend
Your excitement says, "YES"
Your brain says, "When will this end?"
Then suddenly as swift as it began, the ride is over
You grab your partner,
giggle and run
What's coming up next?
On to more fun

GIGGLES!

Giggle, giggle, and giggle
Giggle all day long
Giggle while you're working
or as you sing a song
Giggle when it's funny
Giggle when it's not
Giggle at the rain
or when the weather's hot
Giggle when it's snowing
and you're skiing down the hill
Giggle on the weekday
or if you are feeling ill
Giggling is funny
and it makes you feel real good
Now don't you just feel happy?
Well that's right, you should
Giggles are our blessings,
they're just downright fun
Now go ahead start giggling
until the day is done

TEN TABLESPOONS OF BUTTER

Don't eat ten tablespoons of butter
because if you do,
then those ten tablespoons of butter
will put ten pounds of fat on you
So be careful with that butter
and do not taste the fudge,
or your heart will start to flutter
and your sleek arms will turn to sludge
So throw it in the garbage
and do not eat it now
or you will be so sorry
because you'll look like your pet cow
Moooooo

DREAM WORDS?

Exclamation point!
Comma,
Hyphen-
Words keep on going
Minds never stop
Even though sleep
takes us into bed, plop
Words still live in your brain
Through dreams that start to arise
this time though
Periods. Commas, Exclamation points! Hyphens-
turn into shadows that elongate or frighten
your brain to makes up stories
Long into the night,
sentences scream or run with delight
Words take over the things
that happened yesterday
Warily scathing and climbing and sway
over the cliffs
falling, flying, running away, jumping,
thrilling our brain at night
Keeping our hearts pumping
with thrill at the weirdness
that comes in the mind
When sleep takes over that intense days' grind
Imagine your surprise
when you awake with a start
That exclamation points just end intense words
and this poem is just art

CHEWED-UP CHRISTMAS PRESENT

I was really looking forward to Christmas
Everything was going on cue
The house was all bedecked, cookies smelled good
The tree was all ornamented too
But then I was coming home from work
and what should meet my eyes?
But a chewed-up package in the yard
making me shriek, "Oh what an awful demise"
The dog had chewed up our present,
the one that had come from LA
How could that unkind dog have done that?
The sky turned from blue to gray
I bawled and shed tears in upset
"Oh you terribly terrible pet
you ate over a pound of chocolate
Now I'm going to have to take you to the vet"
Well nothing happened to the puppy,
he luckily came out alright
But I was so sad about our chewed-up Christmas present
That darn dog ruined our night!

ARE YOU SAYING I'M FAT?

Chubbiness will get you
if you're not aware
First you eat some cookies
while you brush your hair
Next the urges hit you
when you're passing through your town
So you stop at the station,
buy and then gobble the goodies down
Then your stomach starts to rumble
half-way through your meeting
Lunch is on your mind
you can only concentrate on eating
What should I have
you wonder during the work-related clause
A Euro sandwich sounds good, you think
as you start to drool through your jaws
The boss asks you a question
and throws a ton of work on your desk
But your mind isn't on it
as you hurry through this working quest
Should I go to Arby's?
McDonald's or Burger King?
Your mind begins to wander
as your phone continues to ring
At last it's time for lunch,
you race to your car
The lights all hit red it seems
and the restaurants are so far
Soon you step through the coveted door,
the lovely smells sink into your whole being
Your tummy growls with hunger
and your eyes want all they are greedily seeing
You order more than you should

and eat until you're stuffed
Then you get up angry with yourself
that your body looks so puffed
The next morning you step on the scale
and scream with all your might
Why, oh why, did I have that triple-cheeseburger,
french-fries, and chocolate shake last night?
Oh, I bet you wish you knew how to stifle
those cravings that overcome your very soul
So that you can begin to lose weight
and reach that fitness goal
So please turn off those hunger cravings
turn away from that full plate
Pass by those gas stations with the donuts
Do it now so you will lose weight

I DON'T WANNA!

"I don't wanna!" shouts the girl
awakening from slumber
Arms stretching high above her head
yawning loudly, rising too soon with dread
Slowly her body moves now
legs sliding toward the edge of her bed
Her hair is a beautiful mess
blond and curly
Her azure eyes awake now
sensing the hurry
She must shower, she must run
"Oh holy crap!" she screams
Her day has begun
The babies are crying
waiting to be changed and fed
The older child still in slumber
lying asleep in bed
Her husband is long gone, away at work
She imagines him happily humming a song
"Why, oh why," she screams,
just wanting to lie back down
absorbed in her perfect dreams
but alas and alors, the day has begun
It's time to get ready
she mustn't sleep anymore
So off she goes to start her day
"I Don't Wanna"
She screams in dismay

THE END

NOTES

FOREWORD

1. "To every thing there is a season, and a time to every purpose under the heaven" (Ecclesiastes 3:1, KJV). Pg. x
2. "Whatever is has already been, and what will be has been before; and God will call the past to account" (Ecclesiastes 3:15, NIV). Pg. x

6. NEVERTHELESS

1. "For, when we were come into Macedonia, our flesh had no rest, but we were troubled on every side; without were fightings, within were fears. Nevertheless God, that comforteth those that are cast down, comforted us" (2 Corinthians 7:5-6, KJV). Pg. 10

10. FAITH IS AN OPEN DOOR

1. "But Thomas, one of the twelve, called Didymus, was not with them when Jesus came. The other disciples therefore said unto him, We have seen the Lord. But he said unto them, Except I shall see in his hands the print of the nails, and put my finger into the print of the nails, and thrust my hand into his side, I will not believe" (John 20:24-25, KJV). Pg. 15
2. "Blessed Assurance" by Fanny Crosby, 1873. Pg. 15

11. FOLLOW YOUR OWN PATH

1. "Be strong and of a good courage, fear not, nor be afraid of them: for the LORD thy God, he it is that doth go with thee; he will not fail thee, nor forsake thee" (Deuteronomy 31:6, KJV). Pg. 16
2. "Jesus saith unto him, I am the way, the truth, and the life: no man cometh unto the Father, but by me" (John 14:6, KJV). Pg. 16

15. I AM

1. "And God said unto Moses, I AM That I AM: and he said, Thus shalt thou say unto the children of Israel, I AM hath sent me unto you" (Exodus 3:14, KJV). Pg. 22
2. "Blessed are they that do his commandments, that they may have right to the tree of life, and may enter in through the gates into the city" (Genesis 3:22-24, NIV). Pg. 22

    "And the LORD God said, 'The man has now become like one of us, knowing good and evil. He must not be allowed to reach out his hand and take also from the tree of life and eat, and live forever.' So the LORD God banished him from the Garden of

Eden to work the ground from which he had been taken. After he drove the man out, he placed on the east side of the Garden of Eden cherubim and a flaming sword flashing back and forth to guard the way to the tree of life" (Revelations 22:14, KJV). Pg. 22

3. "After this manner therefore pray ye: Our Father which art in heaven, Hallowed be thy name. Thy kingdom come, Thy will be done in earth, as it is in heaven. Give us this day our daily bread. And forgive us our debts, as we forgive our debtors. And lead us not into temptation, but deliver us from evil: For thine is the kingdom, and the power, and the glory, for ever. Amen" (Matthew 6:9-13, KJV). Pg. 22
4. "For as the heaven is high above the earth, so great is his mercy toward them that fear him. As far as the east is from the west, so far hath he removed our transgressions from us" (Psalm 103:11-12, KJV). Pg. 22
5. "But because of your stubbornness and your unrepentant heart, you are storing up wrath against yourself for the day of God's wrath, when his righteous judgment will be revealed. God 'will repay each person according to what they have done.' To those who by persistence in doing good seek glory, honor and immortality, he will give eternal life" (Romans 2:5-7, NIV). Pg. 22

16. WHAT ABOUT YOU?

1. "Thomas said to him, 'Lord, we do not know where You are going. How can we know the way?' Jesus said to him, 'I am the way, and the truth, and the life. No one comes to the Father except through me'" (John 14:5-6, NKJV). Pg. 23
2. "And he said unto them, Go ye into all the world, and preach the gospel to every creature" (Mark 16:15, KJV). Pg. 23

18. GOD THE LIFESAVER

1. "And when they were come to the place, which is called Calvary, there they crucified him, and the malefactors, one on the right hand, and the other on the left" (Luke 23:33, KJV). Pg. 26

19. ARE YOU READY?

1. "I pledge allegiance to the Flag of the United States of America, and to the Republic for which it stands, one Nation under God, indivisible, with liberty and justice for all" (The Pledge of Allegiance," 4 USC Sec. 4). Pg. 27
2. "On that same night I will pass through Egypt and strike down every firstborn of both people and animals, and I will bring judgment on all the gods of Egypt. I am the LORD. The blood will be a sign for you on the houses where you are, and when I see the blood, I will pass over you. No destructive plague will touch you when I strike Egypt" (Exodus 12:12-13, NIV). Pg. 27
3. "Now when Daniel knew that the writing was signed, he went into his house; and his windows being open in his chamber toward Jerusalem, he kneeled upon his knees three times a day, and prayed, and gave thanks before his God, as he did aforetime" (Daniel 6:10, KJV). Pg. 27

22. SING TODAY

1. "The LORD is my shepherd; I shall not want. He maketh me to lie down in green pastures: he leadeth me beside the still waters. He restoreth my soul: he leadeth me in the paths of righteousness for his name's sake. Yea, though I walk through the valley of the shadow of death, I will fear no evil: for thou art with me; thy rod and thy staff they comfort me. Thou preparest a table before me in the presence of mine enemies: thou anointest my head with oil; my cup runneth over. Surely goodness and mercy shall follow me all the days of my life: and I will dwell in the house of the LORD forever" (Psalm 23, KJV). *Pg. 32*

26. EVIL "EDNA"

1. "For we brought nothing into this world, and it is certain we can carry nothing out" (1 Timothy 6:7, KJV). *Pg. 36*

28. WHEN I'M AFRAID

1. "For God hath not given us the spirit of fear; but of power, and of love, and of a sound mind" (2 Timothy 1:7, KJV). *Pg. 41*
2. "The LORD himself goes before you and will be with you; he will never leave you nor forsake you. Do not be afraid; do not be discouraged" (Deuteronomy 31:8, NIV). *Pg. 41*
   "Have I not commanded you? Be strong and courageous. Do not be afraid; do not be discouraged, for the LORD your God will be with you wherever you go" (Joshua 1:9, NIV). *Pg. 41*
3. "And after the earthquake a fire; but the LORD was not in the fire: and after the fire a still small voice" (1 Kings 19:12, KJV). *Pg. 41*

29. IN GOD'S ARMS

1. "To every thing there is a season, and a time to every purpose under the heaven" (Ecclesiastes 3:1, KJV). *Pg. 42*

30. STAY FAITHFUL

1. "Blessed assurance, Jesus is mine,
   O what a foretaste of glory divine!
   Heir of salvation, purchase of God,
   Born of His spirit, washed in His blood:
   This is my story, this is my song,
   Praising my Saviour all the day long"
   Blessed Assurance, by Fanny Crosby, 1873. *Pg. 44*

32. TAKE AWAY MY PHARAOH'S HEART

1. "And the LORD God planted a garden eastward in Eden; and there he put the man whom he had formed. And out of the ground made the LORD God to grow every tree that is pleasant to the sight, and good for food; the tree of life also in the midst of the garden, and the tree of knowledge of good and evil" (Genesis 2:8-9, KJV). Pg. 46

33. ONLY BELIEVE

1. "And about the ninth hour Jesus cried with a loud voice, saying, Eli, Eli, lama sabachthani? that is to say, My God, my God, why hast thou forsaken me?" (Matthew 27:46, KJV). Pg. 48
2. "And when they came to the place that is called The Skull, there they crucified him, and the criminals, one on his right and one on his left. And Jesus said, 'Father, forgive them, for they know not what they do'" (Luke 23:33-34, ESV). Pg. 48

39. I LOVE YOU, MOM

1. "Why do you look at the speck of sawdust in your brother's eye and pay no attention to the plank in your own eye? How can you say to your brother, 'Let me take the speck out of your eye,' when all the time there is a plank in your own eye? You hypocrite, first take the plank out of your own eye, and then you will see clearly to remove the speck from your brother's eye" (Matthew 7:3-5, NIV). Pg. 59

ACKNOWLEDGMENTS

To my niece, Angela, for all her hard work in getting this poetry published, thank you!

To my daughter, Kristen, for permission to use her beautiful painting of me on the cover.

www.ingramcontent.com/pod-product-compliance
Lightning Source LLC
Chambersburg PA
CBHW020913080526
44589CB00011B/573